Some definitions of worry:

"An uncomfortable feeling of nervousness."

"Concern about something that might happen."

"Feeling fearful or unhappy because you think something bad will come true."

Which one would you choose to describe your worry?

WHAT'S INSIDE

#1 Intro to worry
#2 What worrying feels like
#3 Different ways to control your worries
#4 Do your best

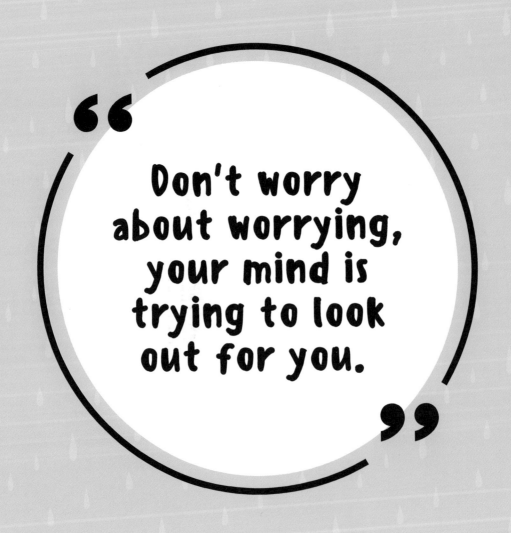

"Don't worry about worrying, your mind is trying to look out for you."

You can't always see when someone's worrying but they definitely <u>do</u>.

Worrying happens
when you try to
imagine
what your future's
going to bring.

But you CAN take control and teach yourself to think positively first.

Worrying doesn't solve problems.

And for the ones that could come true, there's usually a solution you can find.

Worrying doesn't change anything, it just takes your happiness away.

So enjoy the now, let go of control and don't try to predict your day.

Your worry brain is there to warn you if it thinks there's something you shouldn't do...

So don't worry
about worrying,
your mind is trying
to look out for
you.

> When you have worries on your mind, you might feel other emotions too.

What
worrying
feels like

Some common worries that children your age will experience are...

Parents separating

Talking in groups

Starting a new school

"Bad guys"

Weather changes: earthquakes, lightening

Going to the doctor or dentist

Tests e.g. timed maths tests

Getting a new sibling

Falling out with friends

Being left out

Getting poorly or someone you love getting poorly

The dark

School work

New experiences

Moving house

Being away from parents

Do you worry about any of these?

Worrying can make you...

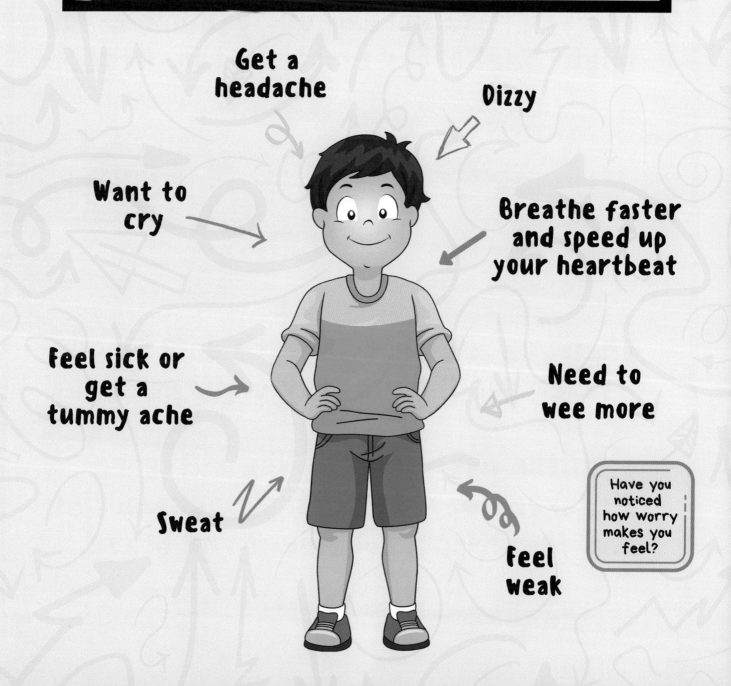

When you have worries on your mind, you might feel other emotions too, like...

Anger

Jealousy

Fear

Sadness

When you are worrying, it's easy to get stuck feeling unhappy or stressed.

In the next chapter you will learn different ways to control your worries and feel happy, confident and brave...

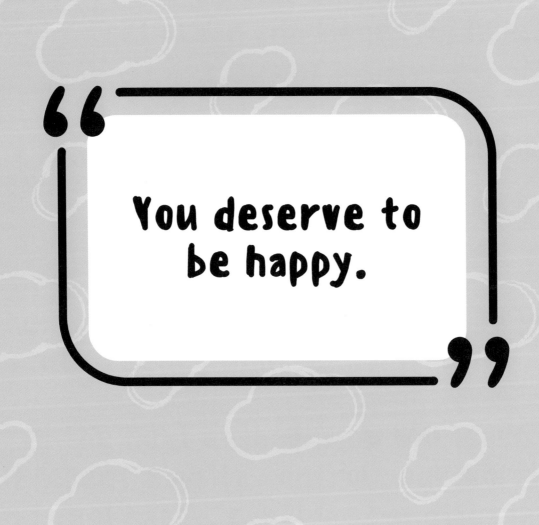

#3

Different ways
to control
your worries

TALK TO YOUR WORRIES

Talk to the worries that come into your head, tell your worry brain you're choosing to be happy instead.

Talking back to your worries can help figure out which ones are true. Pretend you're giving your friend advice and discuss what you could do...

I'm worried I'll have no one to play with at lunch.

Thank you for looking out for me worry brain but...

I'm a kind person and people would be lucky to play with me.

I could always ask for help or enjoy my own company.

Next time a worry pops into your head, have a talk with yourself. Some things you could say are...

"I am brave, I CAN defeat this.."

"How can I handle this in the best way?"

"Is this likely to happen?"

"You are not the boss of me worry brain, I am in control."

"This feeling will pass."

"I CAN share this worry."

"That is NOT true."

"What can I do IF this happens?"

"What will probably happen?"

BE MINDFUL

Mindfulness helps you keep worries away
by focusing your thoughts on the now.
It might sound strange but its super
helpful if you practice how.

It means really concentrating on
whatever you're doing, whether it's
playing, reading, dancing or chewing.

If you're mindful
you won't worry about what the future
might bring,
you'll just be enjoying the moment you're
in.

"Try not to think about what the future might bring but work hard on enjoying the moment you're in."

Use your Imagination

Visit your favourite place inside your mind. How does it feel to be there, what do you see? Smell? Hear? Touch?

Butterfly Breathing

Take some deep breaths, as you breathe in, lift your wings (your arms) up towards the sky. As you breathe out, bring them down gently. Repeat until your worries have fluttered away.

Try out these fun mindful exercises when you next have a worry...

Have a Mindful Hug

Hug someone and keep them close. Notice how it feels...
Can you feel the persons heartbeat?
Hear their breathing?
Smell their shampoo?

Take a Mindful Walk

Take a mindful walk with your family. Try to walk in silence, notice everything around you with all your senses. Do you hear birds, see cars? How does the air feel? What can you smell?

WRITE YOUR WORRIES AWAY

Write down whatever worries you have
on your mind.
Solve them if you can,
then choose to leave them behind.

By emptying your mind
you'll feel light and less tense,
and any worries you have may start
making more sense.

Journal

A journal is the perfect place to write your worries down.

Once written down, you might see the worry differently. You can question the worry and make a plan to deal with it.

A worry jar is a place you can put your worries so they are out of your mind.

Write your worries down on a slip of paper and put them into a jar. You can leave them in there or pick a time to work through them.

Worry jar

My Worries

Worry monster

Write down your worries and feed them to a worry monster who can eat them up...

To create your monster- find a cardboard box, cut a hole for the mouth and make it come to life with eyes, teeth, arms and more.

MAKE AN ACTION PLAN

Worrying doesn't solve your problems
and most worries don't come true.
For the ones that might happen there
is something you could do...

Find the best solution for your worry
and plan for what you can.
Write down the steps you'll take in a
helpful action plan...

If you question your worry and it's something you will have to deal with, making a plan can help you feel brave enough to face it.

My Worry -

Staying overnight for my school trip

My action plan -

- Tell Mum I'm feeling worried about it
- Bring my favourite teddy or toy to remind me of home
- Practice by staying at a family or friends house

FOCUS ON THE POSITIVE

You have the power to control your worries and be positive instead.
Work on having more happy thoughts than worries going on inside your head.

Choose to think about all your worries differently,
flip them into positive thoughts and decide to be HAPPY.

You have the power to change your worries into thoughts that are helpful and kind.

For example

Worries	Instead I can say
I'm going to forget my solo in the dance show.	I will keep practising until I feel more prepared.
I am scared I will get all the questions wrong on my maths test.	I can remain calm, I will celebrate any answers I get correct.

Try this

Imagine your mind as a garden...
The garden is made up of weeds and flowers...

'Worry Weeds'

When you worry you water the weeds.

+

'Positive Posies'

When you think positively you water the flowers.

Every garden has <u>some</u> weeds but you can choose to grow MORE flowers by focusing on the positive. You have the power to make your mind garden beautiful.

LET IT GO

You can't control the future, but you can control how you feel no matter what comes your way.

You can choose to be happy in any situation and tell your worries that they can't stay.

Truly believe you can be happy no matter what is going on around.
Go with the flow, let go of control and true happiness will be found.

Try making a list of what you <u>can</u> control and for anything else try to go with the flow...

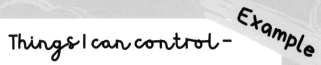

Example

Things I can control -

- How long I spend worrying
- How kind I am to myself
- What I play and who with
- The books I read
- My attitude
- If I ask for help or not

Try me!

Balloon meditation

Find somewhere quiet to sit or lay down and close your eyes.

Take some deep breaths and when you breathe out imagine you are blowing any worries you can't control into a big balloon.

Fill it with one or many.

Imagine letting go of the balloon and watch the worries float far away.

BE KIND TO YOURSELF

Get rid of any worries by treating yourself kind.
Speak to yourself nicely and do what you enjoy to clear your mind.

Instead of feeling down, try showing yourself support.
Remember all emotions pass so be okay with every thought.

Be the 'watcher of your worries'.
Notice your worry and if it can't be solved or isn't true just let it pass through your mind and watch it disappear.

When you look after yourself and show yourself love it's much easier to keep worries away.

Some ways to show yourself love...

Speak kindly to yourself

Do things you enjoy

Drink plenty of water

Get enough sleep

Eat healthy

Get daily exercise outdoors

You deserve to be happy!

TALK IT OUT

Talking through your worries with someone can really help them shrink.

It may be useful to have a worry time each day where you sit down and have a think.

Worries can be solved faster with someone helping you. Finding the best solution can be easier with help deciding what to do.

No one can read your mind, if you want someone's help with a worry then you'll need to be brave and talk to them about it.

Pick a worry time each day to talk through your worries with someone.
Don't focus on your worries until it's time to.
(Pick a time that will have the least interruptions.)

Make sure that the person you want to talk to is available to listen.

> **Use your energy to believe in yourself instead of worrying.**

DO YOUR BEST

Now you've learnt why you might worry, how it feels and what to do. Take control whenever they come your way... you have the power to!

With practice you will keep getting better and better.
If you're struggling, ask a grown-up and work through them together.

Do your best not to stress when worries enter your mind, because you have the power to leave them behind.

Use your energy to *Believe* IN *yourself* instead of worrying.

Make a 'coping kit'

It can be handy to make a list or a 'coping kit' of quick things you can do if you are alone or somewhere busy, like school, to stop a worry taking control.

Some examples

- Say positive words to yourself in your head
- Take some deep mindful breaths
- Count backwards from 100
- Play stop the bus game from A - Z
- Squeeze something and release (squeeze your fists if you have nothing soft or squishy close by)
- Try to remember the words to a song
- Imagine your loved ones cuddling you
- Give yourself a firm hug or fold your arms tightly across your chest
- Focus your mind on your body, tense a muscle and then relax it... work up from your toes to your head

Printed in Great Britain
by Amazon